# MUHAMMAD ALI

Also by Flip Schulke

*Martin Luther King, Jr.: A Documentary . . . Montgomery to Memphis*

*King Remembered* (with Penelope McPhee)

*He Had a Dream: Martin Luther King, Jr., and the Civil Rights Movement*

*Your Future in Space: The U.S. Space Camp Training Program*
(with Penelope McPhee)

*Underwater Photography for Everyone*

# MUHAMMAD ALI

## *The Birth of a Legend,*
## *Miami, 1961–1964*

Flip Schulke

Text by Matt Schudel

St. Martin's Griffin 〼 New York

www.stmartins.com

Book design by James Sinclair

Photos on pages 55 and 144 by Angelo Dundee, © Flip Schulke.

Library of Congress Cataloging-in-Publication Data

Schulke, Flip.
    Muhammad Ali : the birth of a legend, Miami, 1961–1964 / Flip Schulke : text by Matt
Schudel.
      p.  cm.
   ISBN 0-312-20340-3 (hc)
   ISBN 0-312-26360-0 (pbk)
   1. Ali, Muhammad, 1942–  . 2. Ali, Muhammad, 1942–  Pictorial works.
   3. Boxers (Sports)—United States Biography.  4. Boxers (Sports)—United States
Biography Pictorial works.  I. Schudel, Matt.  II. Title.
  GV1132.A44S365  1999
  796.83'092—dc21                                   99-31473
   [B]                                              CIP

First St. Martin's Griffin Edition: February 2001

10 9 8 7 6 5 4 3 2 1

*To Elizabeth Schulke Davidson, PhD,*
*who practices the highest profession—teaching.*
*And to Joe Toreno and Amanda Friedman,*
*who have the passion, the vision, and have caught the Torch.*

# CONTENTS

ACKNOWLEDGMENTS

This pictorial book of the early years of Cassius Clay/Muhammad Ali would not have been possible without the active help of many people.

I am extremely grateful to my literary agent, Jennifer Lyons, who discovered the material for this book among the mass of my journalistic photographs. Her drive got the project going.

Many thanks to my editors at St. Martin's Press, Diane Higgins, Andrew Miller, and Becky Koh, for their suggestions and confidence in all aspects of this book.

A special, heartfelt thanks to Miranda Ford, production editor at St. Martin's Press. She was the spark plug who, through hard work and persistence, brought everything to completion—she cares about Ali as I do.

To James Sinclair, art director, who made the book sparkle; Karen Gillis, production manager, who saw that it was printed beautifully; and to Patricia Fernandez, assistant editor, with whom it was a joy to work.

To John Toreno, who started promoting the book even before all the photographs were selected; right on, kiddo!

To Gerry Astor, picture editor at *Sports Illustrated*, who gave me my first Ali assignment and Phil Kunhardt, assistant picture editor at *Life* magazine, who saw the visual fun in photographing a boxer underwater.

The following people gave long interviews to Matt Schudel, and we thank them all: Angelo Dundee, Ali's lifelong trainer and close friend; Dr. Ferdie Pacheco, the "fight doctor," with whom I had great fun at University of Miami's medical school; Hank Kaplan, boxing historian; Jimmy Ellis, sparring partner and former heavyweight champion; Tony Alongi, sparring partner; and Ingemar Johansson of Sweden, a former heavyweight champion.

As a photographer, I am only as good as the man or woman in the darkroom who prints the negative as I had envisioned it. These men and women often find ways to make the prints much better than my guiding master prints. Therefore, with a deep bow, I would like to thank the following master printers: Ricki Troiano, Wolfram Kloetz, and Vernon Sigl of Modernage Labs, New York City; Andrea Maitland and Kip Cowan of Thomson Labs, Coral Gables, Florida; and Jim Megargee of MV Labs, New York City.

Also, to Ben Chapnick of Black Star Picture Agency, who has provided me with work for all of forty-five years—thanks for always picking up the telephone.

I would hereby like to honor the memory of Howard Chapnick, the former president of Black Star, who always encouraged the pursuit of photography that showcased the very best in people and human nature.

And, finally, to the *greatest* of them all—Muhammad Ali, aka Cassius Clay—who is truly the greatest global role model of the twentieth century. I give my thanks, admiration, and love to a sweet man, who has never forgotten that—in the end—it is the *children* who matter the most.

Photographic prints from this book are available through:

James Danziger
Danziger Gallery
851 Madison Avenue, Second Floor
New York, NY 10021
(212) 734-5300

# CHRONOLOGY

- January 17, 1942: Born in Louisville, Kentucky, as Cassius Marcellus Clay, Jr.
- 1954: Begins to train as amateur boxer in Louisville.
- 1957: Meets trainer Angelo Dundee in Louisville.
- 1958–1959: Wins Golden Gloves amateur tournaments in Louisville, nationwide.
- April 18, 1960: Registers for military draft in Louisville.
- June 1960: Graduates from Central High School, Louisville.
- September 1960: Wins gold medal as light-heavyweight in Olympic Games, Rome.
- October–November 1960: Trains briefly in San Diego with light-heavyweight champion Archie Moore.
- October 29, 1960: First professional fight, versus Tunney Hunsaker, in Louisville.
- December 19, 1960: Arrives in Miami to begin training with Angelo Dundee.
- December 27, 1960: Has second professional fight in Miami Beach; first with Dundee as trainer.
- 1961: Begins attending Nation of Islam temple in Miami.
- September 8, 1961: *Life* magazine article published; first article in national press about Cassius Clay.
- September 25, 1961: *Sports Illustrated* publishes its first article on Cassius Clay.
- 1962: Meets Malcolm X.
- March 9, 1962: Classified 1-A for military draft.

- September 25, 1962: Sonny Liston defeats Floyd Patterson for heavyweight title.
- July 22, 1963: Liston defeats Patterson in rematch.
- February 25, 1964: Cassius Clay defeats Liston for heavyweight title in Miami Beach.
- February 27, 1964: Announces conversion to Nation of Islam.
- March 6, 1964: Elijah Muhammad changes Clay's name to Muhammad Ali.
- March 26, 1964: Reclassified 1-Y ("not qualified") for military draft.
- February 21, 1965: Malcolm X murdered in New York.
- May 25, 1965: Ali defeats Liston in rematch in Lewiston, Maine.
- February 17, 1966: Ali's request for religious deferment from military service denied; reclassified 1-A.
- April 28, 1967: Refuses induction order into military; heavyweight title withdrawn.
- June 20, 1967: Convicted of draft evasion and sentenced to five years in prison; remained free on appeal.
- December 1968: Ali spends week in jail in Miami for driving without a license.
- October 26, 1970: Resumes boxing career, versus Jerry Quarry; trains in Miami Beach.
- March 8, 1971: First fight with Joe Frazier; first professional defeat.
- June 28, 1971: U.S. Supreme Court unanimously overturns Ali's draft-evasion conviction.
- March 31, 1973: Loses to Ken Norton; breaks jaw during fight.
- September 10, 1973: Defeats Norton in rematch.
- January 28, 1974: Defeats Frazier in second fight.
- October 30, 1974: Regains heavyweight title from George Foreman in Zaire.
- October 1, 1975: Defeats Joe Frazier in third fight in Philippines.
- February 15, 1978: Loses title to Leon Spinks.
- September 15, 1978: Defeats Spinks in rematch; regains heavyweight title for third time.
- December 11, 1981: Ali loses final fight to Trevor Berbick; retires from boxing one month before his fortieth birthday.

# Introduction

His may be the most famous face in the world. Even today, two decades after he retired from the hard profession that built his fame, the legend of Muhammad Ali continues to grow. During perhaps the most volatile years of the century—the years of John F. Kennedy, of Dr. Martin Luther King, Jr., and of Vietnam—Ali was the most outspoken, most controversial athlete of his time. Once reviled for what some called his cowardice at refusing to be drafted to fight in Vietnam, Ali is now honored as an avatar of integrity and peace. Denounced in the halls of Congress, stripped of his world championship, and deprived of his profession, Ali would only grow taller in the public mind. Over time, people came to understand that it wasn't fear that kept this fighter from going to war—it was a rare kind of courage. Muhammad Ali has earned his place in our hearts because we now see him for what he has always been: a man of deep and persuasive conviction.

Ali was not the first superstar of American sports, or even of boxing. But he remains one of the rare athletes whose cultural significance reached beyond the arena, beyond America, beyond the boundaries of race and faith.

He rose to prominence as an athlete, then became a cultural hero embraced by all the world. Today, he stands muted within the silent prison of Parkinson's syndrome, a condition almost surely brought on by too many punishing years in the ring. Yet nothing can deny him his dignity. He has become sanctified, anointed as a figure resembling a secular pope. Ali is much more than famous—he is loved. Everyone the world over recognizes his sweet, smiling, un-marked face. He is puffier, perhaps, but not much changed from the way he looked nearly forty years ago, when he was young, full of sass, and brashly telling all who would listen to him that one day he would be champion of the world. He did become that champion, of course—first as a boxer, now as a gentle man of goodwill and peace.

Today, as symbolized by his lighting of the Olympic torch in Atlanta in 1996, Muhammad Ali is accorded the honor and respect of an international ambassador. Yet, after all these years, few people realize that his legend first took shape in the steamy perpetual summer of Miami. It was the place of his apprenticeship and youth, the place where he rose to fame and glory, the place where the world caught its first glimpse of the beautiful boxer who spun out hilarious doggerel about his opponents and himself. They were wild and fantastic tales and, as we look back, they all came true.

"There's no more interesting human being," says his former trainer, Angelo Dundee, "than Muhammad Ali."

Everyone could see that he was a prodigy of boxing, yet those early years—before the championships, before his battles with the authorities, before he was Muhammad Ali—remain the great unknown period of his life. He was, in many ways, an innocent living in a more innocent time.

From the age of twelve, when he first set foot in a gym, he had known that he would become a professional boxer. In September 1960, Cassius Marcellus Clay, Jr., was barely three months out of high school in Louisville, Kentucky, when he won a gold medal in boxing at the Olympic Games in Rome. On the flight home, he wore the medal around his neck. Once he was back on native soil, people were dazzled by more than the gold. He was a brilliant, powerful athlete, of course, but he was also endowed with charisma and star quality, even then.

He was vastly talented and, to fans of boxing at least, already well known. Soon the world would take notice of this young demigod of the ring who was a perfect combination of athletic ability and box-office allure. But he was still only eighteen years old. After the Olympics, a syndicate of eleven blue-blood Louisville businessmen signed on to sponsor and support the young fighter, in return for a share of his winnings. They paid him a bonus of $10,000 and a monthly stipend of $333. Clay moved to San Diego to train with the light-heavyweight champion Archie Moore, but he soon chafed under Moore's stern regimen and headed back to Louisville.

The young Clay—and the Louisville Sponsoring Group—then made the best decision of his career. He went to Miami to learn to be a professional boxer under the skilled hand of Angelo Dundee. Dundee was still in his thirties but had already led three boxers to world titles, and in time he would be almost as legendary a trainer as Ali would be a fighter. Throughout the 1950s, he and his older brother Chris, a tireless promoter, had made Miami Beach second only to New York as the boxing capital of America. Dundee had a stable of flashy young fighters, many of them from Cuba, training at a little second-story sweatbox in Miami Beach called the Fifth Street Gym.

Dundee and Cassius Clay were not strangers, even at that early stage. They had first met in 1957, when Dundee had taken several of his fighters north to Louisville. He was watching television in his hotel room when he received a phone call from the lobby.

"My name is Cassius Marcellus Clay," the boyish voice on the house phone said. "I'm going to be heavyweight champion of the world!"

He was fifteen years old. Dundee invited him to his room, and they talked for four hours. Two years passed, and when Dundee returned to Louisville, the young Clay badgered him for a chance to spar with one of Dundee's professional fighters. Clay stepped in the ring with Willie Pastrano, and it was soon obvious that the seventeen-year-old amateur was getting the better of the skilled Pastrano—who four years later would become light-heavyweight champion of the world.

One year later, in December 1960, Cassius Clay stepped off a train in downtown Miami, and walked straight into history.

"Everybody remembers '64, when he won the title," says Dundee, adding, in typical Angelo-ese: "They don't remember the comeuppance."

Those early years were perhaps the most important—but the least chronicled—of Ali's fabled career. In three extended sessions in the early 1960s, before he became familiar to the world as Muhammad Ali, the young Cassius Clay was captured by the cameras of Flip Schulke, himself a young man trying to leave his mark on the world. Working under contract to *Life* and *Sports Illustrated* magazines, Schulke presented the young Clay in tender, even intimate settings that would never be duplicated. It was a perfect match of camera and subject, as Clay's warm, boyish exuberance beamed directly through the lens to reveal a personality of extraordinary confidence and charisma (Schulke's comments are interspersed throught the text). He would become one of the most widely photographed personages in the world, yet these pictures show him at the very beginning of his journey.

In all, Ali would spend nearly a full decade in Miami. It was the place where he grew to manhood, where he won his fame, where he became a champion, where he became a Muslim, where his legend was born. Miami was the place where Cassius Clay became Muhammad Ali.

*I wanted to get some pictures of Cassius running across the causeway.*
*He would run over it every single day because that's how he did his*
*roadwork. It was in the middle of the day, and it was hot. I asked him if*
*he ran in running shorts, and he said no, because it would look funny.*
*So he just had pants on. They weren't wearing jeans in those days.*
*I had him running back and forth, so I could get the picture.*
*That's the Julia Tuttle Causeway, leading over to Miami Beach.*
*What I wanted was the Miami skyline in the background.*

CHAPTER ONE

# The Fifth Street Gym

In 1960 Miami Beach was still flush with high-rolling glory. It was a city that had been built for pleasure, literally an island unto itself, a mile across Biscayne Bay from the mainland city of Miami proper. It was a dressed-up late-night town of cocktail lounges, nightclubs, and swanky hotels that catered to a fast crowd. It was part New York, part Havana, part Las Vegas, and, in those days, part Deep South.

Well into the 1950s, boxing was one of four most popular sports in the country, after baseball, horse-racing, and college football. At the Miami Beach Auditorium the brothers Dundee, Chris and Angelo, staged a night of fights every week. Angelo trained the fighters, and Chris filled the seats. The Fifth Street Gym, at the sunburned corner of Fifth Street and Washington Avenue, was their headquarters.

"The Dundees may have been the best twosome in boxing history," recalls Hank Kaplan, the foremost historian of boxing, and a frequent visitor to the gym. "Angelo developed fourteen world champions and, during the days Chris was promoting, the Fifth Street Gym was the most active gym in the country."

When eighteen-year-old Cassius Clay climbed the stairs to the Fifth Street Gym, he was enrolling in one of boxing's most exclusive academies. He was in the company of past champions Sugar Ramos, Luis Rodriguez, and Mantequilla Napoles, as well as rising stars Ralph Dupas, Florentino Fernandez, and Willie Pastrano. All were there to learn the not-so-gentle art of boxing from Angelo Dundee.

Before it was torn down in 1993—a parking lot is now in its place—the Fifth Street Gym had a kind of grimy romance, built on spilled sweat and blood and the dreams of a thousand hungry kids. The gym was on the second floor, and the only air-conditioning came from the open windows that let in the subtropical heat, the fumes, and the sounds of the city outside. Around the ring, there were a couple of rows of old theater seats from some long-gone movie house. When termites ate away at the floor, Angelo slapped down plywood that quickly became spotted with drops of sweat and, in places, blood.

*I first met Cassius Clay in August of 1961.* **Sports Illustrated** *approached me because they wanted a portrait of a young boxer in Miami.*
*I had never heard of him, and I had never photographed boxing before.*
*They just said, "Go to the gym and get some pictures of him training.*
*Spend three or four days with him."*
*I fell in love with the guy the minute I met him. He was so much fun.*

It was never a palace, yet at one time or another a veritable Hall of Fame of fighters chose to train there: Sugar Ray Robinson, Sugar Ray Leonard, Jake LaMotta, Sonny Liston, Kid Gavilan, Floyd Patterson, Willie Pep, Emile Griffith, and Roberto Duran. It became a stop on the Miami Beach celebrity tour, as Burt Lancaster, Jim Brown, Jackie Gleason, and all four of the Beatles came by to watch the fighters work out.

"The Fifth Street Gym was the meeting place for the elite of boxing," says Angelo Dundee. "I used to be part and parcel of that gym. There was such warmth to the place."

The spotlight was already shining on the Fifth Street Gym, but it became even brighter when Cassius Clay walked up its steps on December 19, 1960.

"I was there his first day, his very first workout," recalls Kaplan, the boxing historian. "He worked with a tall, lean heavyweight from Hollywood named Tony Alongi."

Cigar-chewing trainers and other gym regulars—the so-called Pugilistic College of Cardinals—stood two rows deep to watch the young Olympic champion in the ring.

"I'll never forget that day," Kaplan continues. "The bell rings, and the sparring session begins. The thing we noticed was that when Tony Alongi threw a punch, Ali would just rear back out of the way. One of the old trainers said, 'This kid's gonna get killed.' I'll never forget it."

What they saw was a style of boxing never before seen in a heavyweight. It was so new, so unorthodox that they didn't know what to make of it. Clay held his hands low, around his hips, instead of protecting his face. His peripheral vision, foot speed, and instincts were so acute that he didn't have to block his opponent's punches; he simply dodged them.

"He had clever feet, fast hands," adds Kaplan. "He was the most innovative heavyweight of all time."

Dundee taught Clay how to hit what boxers call the "speed bag" in a fast, steady rhythm to improve his hand-eye coordination and quickness. He could tell without looking when Clay was working out on either the speed bag or the heavy bag.

"It was beautiful," he says. "*Snap, pop, snap! Snap-snap!* The 'snake lick' we used to call it. We gave 'em monikers."

There were other qualities besides Clay's boxing skills that were just as remarkable, especially in someone so young. He was funny and amiable, and he had the handsome, unblemished features of a hero sculpted from marble.

"He was simply the most unusually well-developed athlete that I've ever seen," says Ferdie Pacheco, the "fight doctor" who worked in Clay's corner and treated him at his Miami medical clinic. "He was a perfect physical specimen."

Even in the beginning, before the reporters and TV cameras crowded around him, Clay talked of how "pretty" he was, and everyone could see that it was no idle boast.

"He loved his body," Kaplan recalls. "He loved to look in the mirror and see his sweat hitting the floor as he was jumping rope. Nobody had to push him in the gym."

Clay usually spoke in quiet tones, but when a reporter came into the room he would shout in a high-pitched voice, versifying on the spot. He had charm—rare among boxers—and an infectious humor that drew people in.

"He had me cracking up all the time," Kaplan adds. "The combination that composed Cassius Clay was so unique. He had great athletic ability and comedic ability, and he loved to be onstage. It was an incredible combination."

Other boxers at the Fifth Street Gym called him "Cash" and didn't resent his braggadocio because they knew how hard he worked. In those early years, he was up at 5:00 A.M., running on the streets of Overtown, the black section of Miami where he lived. The Fifth Street Gym was across a causeway at the south end of Miami Beach, a good five miles from Clay's Overtown home. He ran there every day across the Julia Tuttle Causeway, wearing long pants and black lace-up paratrooper boots. At the end of his workouts, which lasted three to four hours, he ran back. He wore a T-shirt boldly emblazoned with his name.

"Many a time I got a call from the police," says Angelo Dundee. " 'Who's that tall, skinny guy? He says he's your fighter.' I said, 'He is. That's Cassius Clay.'

"He ran like a deer. He would never wait for a ride. Never had a car then, early on. He'd come in, he wouldn't be taking a breath. This was the big thing everybody missed on this kid. Hard worker. First guy in the gym, last guy to leave."

"Sometimes I'd say, 'Ali, I'm going over in ten minutes,' " recalls Ferdie Pacheco, whose clinic was in Overtown. " 'Just wait for me a minute.' He'd say, 'No, no, I want to get my work in.' "

He didn't drink, smoke, or, in the early years, chase women. (Later on, they literally lined up at his door.)

"He lived a spartan life," says Kaplan, the boxing historian. "He was very clean-living, kind of a shy kid. I remember I was standing on a street corner in Overtown talking with him, and I was about to light a cigarette. He pulled the cigarette out of my mouth and said, 'You know you shouldn't be smoking.' He pulled a pen out of my pocket and wrote his name on the cigarette—'Cassius Clay'—and he said, 'You keep this. It's going to be worth a lot of money someday.' "

It now rests in a museum in Louisville.

"The confidence and cockiness were so evident from the beginning," says Kaplan. "I'm telling you, he's a remarkable guy."

*We went to the Fifth Street Gym on Miami Beach, and it was like a
dumpy gym. It was upstairs and smelled like a high-school gym. It was a
small place. Angelo Dundee was there (above, behind Clay), and he was
very accommodating. He never restricted photographers, because there
weren't many up there. It was visually colorful because they had painted
5TH STREET GYM in the windows, and it was bright red. I loved it.
I thought this was a great place to make pictures.*

*He had T-shirts made up with his name on the front—CASSIUS CLAY.*
*No one did that kind of self-advertising in those days.*
*I wish I had asked him for one, but I didn't.*

*On the afternoon I arrived to take portraits, Cassius wasn't scheduled*
*to do any sparring. The gym was empty, except for one other boxer.*
*Usually, at the gym, Cassius was joking and having a good time,*
*but on that day he was serious and focused.*

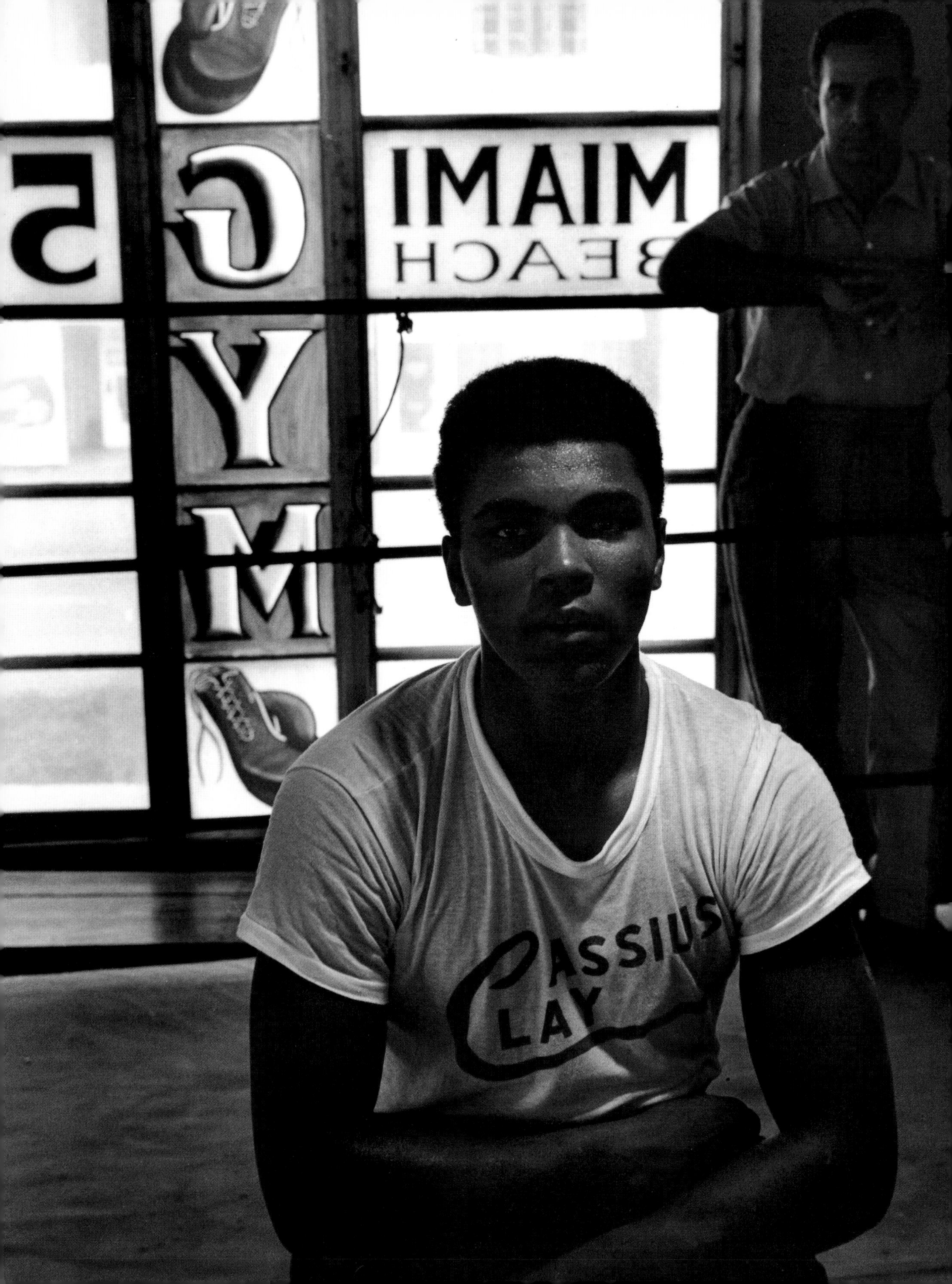
MIAMI
BEACH
CASSIUS
CLAY

*I knew all about Angelo Dundee before he got together with Cassius;*
*he and his brother, Chris, were famous in Miami for promoting fights.*
*Angie was very cooperative and was always kind of in the background.*
*Cassius trusted him completely—they had a very close relationship.*
*Angie wasn't at all taken aback by Cassius's clowning around and*
*he never showed an ounce of racial prejudice.*

# CHAPTER TWO

# Overtown

Angelo Dundee rented a room for Clay at the Alexander Apartments, next to the Famous Chef restaurant, on Northwest Second Avenue in Miami's Overtown. Over time, he would also live at the Mary Elizabeth Hotel, the Sir John Hotel, and in a modest wooden house, all in or near Overtown.

At that time, Overtown—so named because it was "over the tracks"—was the primary black section of Miami. Until it was sliced apart by construction for Interstate 95 in the late 1960s, Overtown was a thriving, self-contained community of shops, restaurants, and professional offices. People came and went at all hours of the day and night. Overtown was Miami's version of Harlem. This was the world in which the teenaged Cassius Clay found himself.

At the time, Miami Beach was the nation's leading tourist destination, and many prominent black entertainers performed at hotels and nightclubs on the Beach. Yet, because of their race, they were not allowed to stay at the ritzy hotels lining Collins Avenue, so every night after their shows, they shuttled back across the causeway to the black hotels of Overtown, most of which had busy nightclubs. It wasn't unusual to see late-night appearances by Ella Fitzgerald, Count Basie, Dinah Washington, or Nat "King" Cole. Northwest Second Avenue became known as Miami's "Little Broadway," and it was the only part of the city where nightclub audiences were integrated.

Overtown began just a couple of blocks north of Flagler Street, the central thoroughfare of Miami's downtown business district. At the end of the century, Miami has become a polyglot city with people of all backgrounds, accents, and hues. In the early 1960s, however, it was a stronghold of Jim Crow, as segregated by law as any backwater burg of Old Dixie. African Americans attended separate schools, stepped to the back of the bus, and drank from "Colored Only" water fountains. Overtown was only a ten-minute walk from Flagler Street, yet they were worlds apart. In many ways, Miami was a subtropical Louisville. When he was not allowed to try on a shirt at Burdines, Miami's largest department store, Clay simply shrugged and moved on. It was what white people had taught him to expect.

Clay trained for three or four hours a day at the Fifth Street Gym in Miami Beach. The rest of the time he spent in Overtown. Everyone in the neighborhood seemed to know him. He took his meals at the Famous Chef, shadowboxed on the streets, flirted with high-school girls, and clowned with the local kids. His eyes and ears were open to the vibrant scene around him, and as day faded into night, the crowds on the streets became ever more dubious.

"The hardest part of the training," a precociously mature Clay said at age nineteen, "is the loneliness. I can't go out in the street and mix with the folks . . . 'cause they wouldn't be out there if they was up to any good. . . . Here I am, surrounded by showgirls, whiskey, and nobody watching me. All this temptation and me trying to train to be a boxer. It's something to think about."

On his walks around Overtown, he met a few members of the Nation of Islam, a Muslim sect then gaining prominence among American blacks, largely through the speeches and writings of Malcolm X. Clay had known of the Muslims as early as 1959, when he returned from a boxing tournament in Chicago with a recording of speeches by Elijah Muhammad, the Nation's longtime spiritual leader.

The Muslims preached a message of racial separation, black pride, self-sufficiency, and clean living that appealed to Clay. He had been raised a Baptist in Louisville, but in early 1961, soon after his arrival in Miami, he visited the Nation of Islam's mosque in Overtown.

"The first time I felt truly spiritual in my life," he would say later, "was when I walked into the Muslim temple in Miami."

Several of his Muslim cronies began to hang out at the Fifth Street Gym, but within that sweaty secular temple, only the timeworn rituals of boxing were honored. Angelo Dundee, to his credit, kept his eyes focused on what happened inside the ring, not outside it.

"Two things I never involve myself in with a fighter," he says, "are his personal life and his religion."

*I went to his room, which was on the ground floor of the Sir John Hotel,*

*right by the pool. The very first time I saw his Olympic gold medal,*

*it was on the counter of his bureau.*

*A lot of the gold had worn off because he handled it so much.*

*He stuck it in his pocket, he showed it to everybody, he put it on himself,*

*he put it around people's necks. He said, "Do you want to try it on?"*

*He took it everywhere we went.*

*Later, there were stories that he'd thrown it off a bridge into the water,*

*but I saw it. He had it with him all the time.*

*His room was next to the Famous Chef restaurant,*

*where he had all his meals. The girls flirted with him all the time.*

*At our first luncheon [in 1961], before we got into the photography,*

*I talked to Cassius about Martin Luther King, because I had been doing*

*a lot of pictures of him. I said, "This guy's fantastic, and I'd love to get*

*you two together. I think King will really like you."*

*I'll always remember—he wasn't angry or anything, he was just being*

*honest—he said, "I'm a boxer, and I really don't want anything to do*

*with the civil-rights program at this time."*

*Now, he didn't turn it down, because the next time I saw King,*

*I told him I had done a story on a boxer and I thought it would really be*

*good for him to know this guy because young people liked him so much.*

*He said, "Flip, boxing is violence.*

*No matter how nice the guy is, it's still violence."*

*I myself think what happened was that Malcolm X saw the advantage of*

*having Cassius join the Muslims. From everything I heard, he catered to*

*him, saying, "You're a great man, you'd be wonderful for us.*

*Islam is a great religion."*

*I can understand King's viewpoint because he was into nonviolence. And*

*Cassius was a boxer. No matter how nice a guy you are, you're bruising*

*someone and trying to knock out another human being for sport.*

*He looked so young and innocent—I mean, he was only nineteen. He loved to kid around, but his normal speaking voice was low and gentle.*

Cassius said he'd analyzed other sports figures; he mentioned that his
heroes were Sugar Ray Robinson, the boxer, and Gorgeous George—a
wrestler who wore a costume and had long, dyed blond hair.
He said, "Gorgeous George was a mediocre wrestler, but with that crazy
costume on, everyone wanted to come to see him. I'll do something like
that. I'm going to recite poetry, and they're going to think I'm nuts."

*In his room, I noticed his clothes were hung on a bar.*

*There was no closet. He had very little hanging there,*

*and I said to him, "I have an expense account.*

*Why don't we go shopping? What about shirts?*

*Why don't we go to Burdines [a major Miami department store]?"*

*So we went in, and there were these shirts for sale. That was the first*

*thing we looked at. You can see in the picture that they were $2.99.*

*He said, "I'm not sure these would fit me."*

*So the salesclerk came over, and he said, "You can't try them on." Some*

*assistant manager came down, and he said that it was a policy—black*

*people could not try on clothing. He would have said "Negroes."*

*Nobody said "black people" in those days.*

*I said, "I can't believe this. This is a big store.*

*I want to talk to the manager."*

*Then the manager came down, and I said I was with*

**Sports Illustrated** *and that we were just trying to get a story.*

*I said, "Listen, this man won an Olympic gold medal."*

*He said, "It doesn't matter." Then he took me aside and said,*

*"Look, we have these rules, and they're the policy of the store.*

*Negroes can't try anything on."*

CLEARANCE

FAMOUS MAKER
SHORT SLEEVE SPORT SHIRTS

2.99

*Once in a while they could try a jacket on because they can slip that on over a shirt. But a shirt's against your skin.*

*I was doing all this civil-rights photography then, and I got very angry. This was on Flagler Street in downtown Miami! Miami was not a city known for segregation, but everything was segregated.*

*Then Cassius came over and said, "Come on, Flip, don't worry about it. I don't want to make a big mess here. It's not that big a deal."*

*I thought in my own mind, Well, he's gone through this so much that he's just learned not to make a fuss.*

*I wanted to get out of there. I thought I might say something. I would have known if he was angry; but Cassius wasn't angry. He was kind of calming me down. I've got a voice that raises easy. I was really teed off because I had been doing a lot of stories with Martin Luther King and other civil-rights stuff. And I thought, My God, this guy has just won the gold medal, and he can't try on a shirt in a store in downtown Miami. It was only a quarter mile away, within walking distance of Overtown, where he was living.*

*So we went to a black store. Cassius had mentioned that he'd really like to*
*have some nice shoes, but in the white stores blacks were required to wear*
*special thick socks when trying on shoes, which made finding*
*the right size practically impossible. So we bought shoes for him in*
*Overtown as well. In the picture to the right, the old army boot was his—the*
*only pair of shoes I ever saw him wear. Naturally, he had to use them for*
*everything, including running. Typically, showing his innate*
*desire to stand out in a crowd, Cassius chose to buy the two-tone wing tips.*

# CHAPTER THREE

# An Arc of Bubbles

In early 1961, a Swedish boxer named Ingemar Johansson was training in Fort Lauderdale for his third heavyweight championship fight with Floyd Patterson. The hard-hitting Swede had won the championship from Patterson in 1959, but the following year Patterson knocked out Johansson to regain his title. One day during training, Johansson came to Miami and staged a short sparring session with nineteen-year-old Cassius Clay at the Fifth Street Gym. People who were there that day have never forgotten what they saw.

"I'll go dancin' with Johansson," chanted Clay.

Antics like that were not just bold; they were strange and unheard-of. Before Ali, boxers seldom boasted. They simply went about their cold business. They attacked with their fists, not their mouths.

But anyone could see that the teenage Ali had something more than exceptional talent; he had supreme confidence, bordering on gall. He dared to taunt a man who, less than a year before, had been the heavyweight champion of the world.

"I should be fighting Patterson, not you," he said. "Come and get me, sucker. Come on, what's the matter, can't hit me?"

The trash-talking would have meant nothing if Ali hadn't backed up his words with his fists and his feet. He was so agile in the ring that he could dart away from the lunging, slow-footed Johansson, while peppering the ex-champion with punches.

Johansson, who still lives part of the year in Florida, has warm memories of the young Ali—but he now claims the two never sparred.

"He's a nice person," he says. "He talked a lot, but you take it with a smile."

One of the people who watched the spectacle that day didn't forget what happened. He was Gil Rogin, a writer for *Sports Illustrated*.

"I'd never seen anything like it before," he said later, "and I've never seen anything like it since."

Clay was more than a boxer of superior skill. He was a fresh, compelling presence in a grim, grunting game. Rogin told his editors in New York about the boastful young boxer, and *Sports Illustrated* assigned its first story about Clay. The photographer who drew the assignment was a Miami freelancer named Flip Schulke.


A native of Minnesota, Schulke had been in Miami since 1954, building a reputation as a photojournalist with an extraordinary eye. In Havana, when Castro seized power in January 1, 1959, Schulke caught the revolutionary leader at the precise moment a white dove landed on his shoulder in the middle of a speech. He photographed wars, the Berlin Wall, astronauts, and auto races. On November 22, 1963, he was the only photographer to get a picture from the sixth-floor window of the Texas School Book Depository, soon after Lee Harvey Oswald had peered down the sight of his rifle through the same window. It's an eerie image, in which you can see boxes stacked to allow a clear shot at the road below.

Schulke became best known, though, for his pictures of the civil-rights movement. He had met Martin Luther King, Jr., in Miami in 1958, and the two young men—still in their twenties, just a year apart in age—became good friends. Schulke chronicled the life-and-death drama of the civil-rights movement throughout the South, once shooting photos on the campus of the University of Mississippi through teargassed eyes. Among the 500,000 photographs he would take over the years were 11,000 of Dr. King and the Southern civil-rights movement.

Schulke had sold his first pictures to *Life* magazine in 1956, but he had never photographed a boxer until he met Cassius Clay in 1961.

He spent five days with the nineteen-year-old Clay. He drove alongside him on the causeway, photographing those long midday runs beneath the hot Miami sun. He shot portraits in the gym, where Clay joked and carried on like a comedian. He ate with him at the Famous Chef. He went to his simple room and saw his Olympic gold medal on the dresser, its gold plate worn through to the silver metal beneath. At Clay's urging, Schulke put it around his neck. Noticing that Clay had few clothes, Schulke took him shopping on the *Sports Illustrated* expense account, only to see him refused service because of the color of his skin.

Schulke told Clay he specialized in underwater photography and had recently published pictures in *Life* of a water-skier shot from below. During one of their lunches, Clay mentioned that he worked out every day in a swimming pool. He said an old trainer had told him that water resistance would add strength to his arms and quickness to his punches. His workouts in the pool, he said, made him the fastest heavyweight around.

A couple of days later, Schulke brought his scuba tank and underwater equipment to the Sir John Hotel, where Clay was staying. He shot pictures as Clay stepped into the pool and went through his routine, throwing punches from different angles, his fists parting the water in an arc of bubbles. At one point, Clay sank to the floor of the pool, his eyes wide open, assuming the stance of a classic hero. Dundee, his trainer, stayed poolside with a towel, rubbing Clay's shoulders when he climbed out. Both Clay and Dundee acted as if it were all a part of a normal day's work.

On September 8, 1961, *Life* magazine ran two pages of Schulke's photographs showing Clay in the water, the bubbles streaming behind his punches. It was the first time he had been featured in a national, general-interest magazine. And it was all a big—but convincing—ruse.

"He couldn't swim!" Dundee explains with a burst of laughter. "This was strictly a gimmick. The idea was to do something that would create some interest, would get the PR."

It was the first and last time Clay ever worked out in a pool. But it would not be the last time he would use quick thinking to his shrewd advantage.

*In the restaurant he said, "I want to get into Life."*

*I said, "I really don't know how I can get you into Life."*

*He said, "Can't you come up with something?*

*Can't you come up with something?"*

*The next day, when I arrived at the Sir John Hotel in Overtown,*

*Clay spontaneously jumped in the pool. I didn't think of the idea.*

*He was just paddling around, but he did a couple of punches.*

*I remember saying to him, when he did that, it was just like the bubbles*

*you could see from underneath in the underwater waterskiing*

*pictures I had just shot for Life. I said, "That's really dramatic."*

*Right there in the pool, he said, "Oh, I do this all the time.*

*I get up in the morning, and I get in the pool and I exercise."*

*I said, "What gave you that idea?" He's a young kid to me,*

*remember, even though I was only thirty-one then.*

*He said, "There's an old trainer who told me that water against your*

*fist creates pressure that's just like a weight."*

*That's when the idea hit me. Everything he said was plausible,*

*and I just swallowed it hook, line, and sinker. I said, "Do a couple more."*

*At the end of the day I called SI and said, "Put me on for a couple more*

*days, so I can take my tank and go down in the pool and get these*

*underwater pictures." That's when the picture editor said,*

*"No. That's crazy."*

*He said, "I don't think I'm ever going to give you a boxer again.*

*People don't shoot boxers laughing and smiling. It's a serious business.*

*He's a heavyweight. And now you're looking at a boxer in the water?*

*That's ridiculous."*

*I called Phil Kunhardt, the assistant picture editor at Life,*

*and Phil said, "I think that's a great idea. You're on for two days."*

*I called up Cassius and we went the next day to do the underwater*

*pictures. I packed everything up, my scuba tank,*

*my underwater camera, and I was so excited*

*to do all this that I forgot my bathing trunks.*

*When I went to get undressed, Cassius said, "Just wear mine."*

*I'll always remember saying to him, "They're never going to fit me,"*

*because I was really skinny in those days.*
*I was like a rail; I weighed about 140 pounds.*
*Then he said, "Look at this little waist"—he would kind of mimic*
*Flip Wilson in a high-pitched voice. He wanted a picture of me*
*wearing his boxing trunks to show that this skinny guy*
*had the same size waist that he had.*
*I ended up shooting the story in Everlasts.*
*In all the pictures, his head is above the water when the picture*
*shows his fist. You're looking at his face through the water, but sometimes*
*he stuck his head down in the water to look at me. I don't remember*
*any conversation except trying to position his fists.*
*I didn't know anything about boxing, to be honest. I never followed it.*
*I just said, "Do all the different punches you do when you're training."*
*For the picture of him standing on the bottom of the pool, he just sank*
*down and stood on the bottom. It's hard to do. I didn't ask him to do it,*
*I didn't put any weights on him or anything.*
*He exhaled all of his air—that's the only way you can sink down.*
*I learned later that Phil Kunhardt decided, if the pictures were good,*
*to get the story in the magazine before the SI story. In those days, Life*
*loved to beat out its sister publication. They went out of their way to*
*do the same story, but do it better. That's exactly what happened.*
*[Life published the pictures of Clay working out in the pool on*
*September 8, 1961; the Sports Illustrated feature ran on September 25.]*
*After he won the championship, I went back to Cassius's house to*
*photograph him again. He pulls out a scrapbook and opens it up and*
*says to the guys around the house, "This guy did the first stories on me."*
*Then he hit the Life story, and that's when he said, "Boy, I really fooled*
*you." The minute he said that, I realized this whole thing was a put-on.*
*He said, "You were so excited about those waterskiing pictures that I*
*figured I could make up the whole story."*
*Boy, to con Life magazine! I never had an inkling that I had been taken.*
*And I love it, because it shows how bright he is. He stayed consistent; if I*
*had detected that this whole thing was faked, I would never have gone*
*with it. Good God, at nineteen years old, to figure something like that out.*
*To me, it shows his genius.*

Clay throwing a left jab (above) and a right cross (right) in the pool of the
Sir John Hotel in Miami, August 1961.

The fluid strength of Cassius Clay.

Underwater bubbles reveal the path of Clay's left jab (left) and left hook (above).

A weak, playful punch (top left) gives way to a variety of well-executed underwater blows.

Flip Schulke, the photographer, with the young Cassius Clay; Angelo
Dundee, Clay's trainer, took the photo.

# CHAPTER FOUR

# The Pinnacle

From 1961 to 1964, Cassius Clay climbed into the first rank of heavyweight contenders with an unbroken string of nineteen victories. But if he wanted to become heavyweight champion, as he had promised himself and the world since his early teens, he would have to go through the formidable roadblock of Sonny Liston.

Liston was the most menacing, most merciless fighter of his time, or perhaps any time. He had a withering glare, a perpetual scowl, powerful, tree-trunk arms, and devastating power in both hands. Charles "Sonny" Liston was one of twenty-four children born to an Arkansas sharecropper; he had grown up in dire rural poverty and deprivation. He could not read or write. After migrating to St. Louis in his teens, he embarked on a life that escalated from street fights to thievery to armed robbery. He learned to box in the Missouri State Penitentiary.

When he entered prison in 1950, Liston said he was twenty, but at least one newspaper recorded his age as twenty-two. When he was released in 1952 and began his boxing career, he gave his birthdate as May 8, 1932. Many people thought he was four to ten years older than he claimed.

When he wasn't beating up men in the ring, he was beating them up on the streets as a legbreaker for the St. Louis labor rackets and mob. In 1957 he went back to jail for nine months after punching out a cop in an alley, leaving him with a gash in his face, a broken arm, and a broken kneecap.

In all, Liston would be arrested a hundred times, leaving him with a reputation that could serve him well in only two professions: crime and boxing. When he was out of jail again in 1958, he flattened one opponent after another.

Finally, on September 25, 1962, he met the reigning heavyweight champion, Floyd Patterson, in Chicago. It took just two minutes and six seconds for Liston to knock him out. Patterson was so ashamed of his performance that he left Chicago disguised behind a fake beard.

They met again on July 22, 1963, in Las Vegas, but the second fight was even more decisive than the first. Liston floored Patterson twice, and after two minutes and ten seconds, it was all over.

Watching that night, from seats near the ring, were Cassius Clay and Angelo Dundee. By then, Clay was the top-ranked contender and for nearly a year he'd been plotting a way to beat Liston. He knew that Liston, toughened by prison and the streets, was afraid of no one—no one, that is, who was sane. Clay decided to play with Liston's mind, to mock him, and to call him names. He would be an irritant, a flake, a nut—anything to make Liston think he was about to fight a man who was literally crazed.

In a Las Vegas casino a couple of days before Liston's fight with Patterson, Clay taunted Liston for losing money at the gaming tables.

"Look at that big ugly bear!" Clay shouted.

"We were chasing him around the casino," Dundee recalls, "and he's at the table shooting craps with his death-look stare."

Liston stood up and profanely threatened to tear Clay's tongue out of his mouth and put it in a different cavity of his body. Some accounts state that he then slapped Clay across the face, but Dundee recalls that Liston "pulled out a pop pistol and shot at us. We ran out of there."

Immediately after he had demolished Patterson, Liston noticed Clay at ringside.

"[Liston] comes by, puts his arm around [Clay]," Dundee recalls, "and he says, 'Don't you get hurt, little boy. We're going to make a lot of money. I'm going to beat you like I'm your *daddy*'"

" 'You'll beat me?' [Clay] says. 'I'm going to beat *you*.' "


During an earlier visit to Las Vegas, in June 1961, Clay discovered a flair for showmanship that would set him apart from everyone else in his sport. He was there to fight a big Hawaiian named Duke Sabedong, but it wasn't the boxer who impressed him most—it was a flamboyant pro wrestler who went by the name of Gorgeous George.

Then famous, now all but forgotten, Gorgeous George was all business—

show business, that is. Part Liberace, part Dennis Rodman, and part thug, George paraded to the ring in flowing satin and silver lamé robes, trimmed in sequins and fur. His hair was bleached a starlet's blond and rolled up in curlers. A valet removed George's robe, dramatically combed his hair out to shoulder-length, then spritzed him with cologne from a huge atomizer. A second lackey made a show of dousing the ring with bug spray. The crowd hooted and booed, a little thrilled and a little repelled at this blend of effeminacy and brawn. But every seat was filled.

"Two days before the fight," Dundee recalls, "we did a TV show, and Gorgeous George is naturally carrying the program—glib, sharp. He said things like, 'I'm going to wrestle this youngster, break his arm off and hit him over the head with it'—that kind of adjective. [Cassius] is listening to the guy, and he's loving it.

"We go to the wrestling show that night—sold out, twelve thousand people. Then we fought the next night, and we had twelve hundred people. So [Cassius] started picking up the syllables and the adjectives as he went along. He got glibber, sharper. He was impressed with this guy and his elocutionary thing."

George often proclaimed that no one could beat him because he was "the greatest wrestler in the world." Privately he told Clay to play up the bragging and self-promotion because, the more outrageous he seemed, the more people would pay to see him fight.

Early in his career, Clay had already been dubbed "The Louisville Lip," "Gaseous Cassius," and "Cash the Brash." He had always been witty and quick with a quip and, since his days as an Olympian, had been spouting doggerel rhymes to his own glory:

> *To make America the greatest is my goal,*
> *So I beat the Russian, and I beat the Pole,*
> *And for the U.S.A. won the Medal of Gold.*
> *Italians said, "You're greater than the Cassius of old."*

After he met Gorgeous George, Clay's fountain of words became a geyser.

"Coming from him, a big, good-looking heavyweight," says Dundee, "it was different. It wasn't good poetry—it was bad poetry. A lot of it was my own."

At the Fifth Street Gym, Clay kept up a steady patter, predicting the rounds in which his opponents would fall. Bemused reporters filled their notebooks with what too many of them considered mere comedy.

"Where do you think I'd be next week if I didn't know how to shout and holler and make the public take notice?" Clay once said. "I'd be poor and I'd probably be down in my hometown, washing windows or running an elevator and saying 'yassuh' and 'nawsuh' and knowing my place."


As Clay won more fights, he won more money. He could buy his own clothes now, plenty of them, and he bought a red Cadillac, in which he cruised around Miami. He liked to drive fast.

"He always wanted a tomato-red Cadillac," Dundee recalls, "and I found out why. Sugar Ray Robinson had a tomato-red Cadillac. He always wanted a house, with a cook. We did that. The Louisville group listened to what I had to say. The tomato-red Cadillac—I told them it's a good investment."

Most memorable of all, Clay bought a broken-down thirty-passenger bus, which he made over as his personal carnival wagon. CASSIUS CLAY ENTERPRISES was painted grandly above the side windows; below, in multi-hued paint, was the legend WORLD'S MOST COLORFUL FIGHTER. He took it all over the country, often at the wheel himself, and made it part of the arsenal in his psychological warfare against Liston. Later, before his championship fight, Clay had another slogan painted on the side: SONNY LISTON WILL GO IN EIGHT.

By 1963, Liston was living in Denver, and Clay and a few friends decided to pay him a visit. Driving the rickety bus cross-country, they got to Denver in the middle of the night. Nevertheless, Clay called the local papers and radio stations, inviting everyone to Liston's house. (He would always be his own best press agent.) He had stocked the bus with a dozen handheld placards: WE ALL LOVE CASSIUS CLAY, MARCH ON LISTON'S CAMP, and BEAR HUNTIN'!

Clay sent a friend to ring the doorbell. Woken from sleep, Liston understandably was not in the best mood. Clay stood on the sidewalk, shouting that he'd whip "the ugly old bear"—then and there, if he had to—as a crony stayed on the bus, honking the horn all the while.

Dundee, who stayed in Miami, loved the idea of the surreal scene: "When they told me they were going to do it, I said, 'Great! I think it's fantastic.'

"They were the fun days—'60 to '64," recalls Dundee, practically singing with glee. "Look at the fun we had, good God Almighty!"


On November 5, 1963, Cassius Clay signed a contract to meet Sonny Liston for the heavyweight title on February 25, 1964. The fight would be held at the Miami Beach Convention Hall, just twelve blocks from the Fifth Street Gym.

When Liston arrived in Miami for training, Clay was at the airport to greet his airplane. "Big ugly bear! I'm gonna whup you right now!" he taunted.

Clay followed Liston's car out of the airport, until Liston pulled off to the side and stormed back to confront Clay. They almost had their first fight right there, on the side of a road in Miami.

Liston's training camp was in Surfside, a beachfront town five miles north of the Fifth Street Gym. The champion went through the motions, but he didn't train too hard because he thought he didn't have to. Gamblers were making bets not just on the outcome of the fight, but on which round Liston would knock out Clay. Joe Louis, the revered heavyweight champion of the 1930s and '40s, was in Liston's camp, more or less to tell everyone that Clay had no chance.

Down at the Fifth Street Gym, Clay was holding court, living up to his own billing as the world's most colorful fighter.

"Round eight to prove I'm great!" he repeated. "I'm gonna put that ugly bear on the floor, and after the fight I'm gonna build myself a pretty home and use him as a bearskin rug."

With the editorial help of Dundee and Drew "Bundini" Brown, Clay recited elaborate poems, including one that could be considered his masterpiece. After a round-by-round description, he reached this vivid conclusion:

*Who would have thought,*
*When they came to the fight,*
*That they'd witness the launching*
*Of a human satellite.*
*Yes, the crowd did not dream,*
*When they laid down their money,*
*That they would see*
*A total eclipse of the Sonny.*

People laughed, but many old-line reporters were offended by Clay's clowning. They thought he lacked gravity, that he was merely a joke and nothing more. Few people looked past the japery into the ring itself.

During his workouts, Clay was focused and intense. When Flip Schulke returned to the Fifth Street Gym in February 1964, he discovered that the blithe, free-spirited teenager he had met two and a half years earlier had filled out and become a powerful, focused man of twenty-two. His maturity showed in his face and in his serious sense of purpose. He had gained twenty pounds of strength without losing any speed. The boyish face was now steely and watchful.

Clay shadowboxed before a mirror propped against the wall, above which was a poster made for the 1962 film *Requiem for a Heavyweight*. For playing a bit part in the movie Clay came away with $500 and a poster that read CASSIUS CLAY VS. MOUNTAIN RIVERA—the name of the aging fighter played by Anthony Quinn.

On February 14, a closed-circuit press conference was held at both training camps. Clay popped off with his usual barbs, using a line that would endure as an apt description of his fighting style: "I float like a butterfly and sting like a bee!"

Schulke was at Liston's camp, and on that day it was the champion who seemed to have caught the bragging bug. As he watched his young challenger on television, Liston joined the verbal joust.

"When the bell sounds," he said, "I'm expectin' for Clay to jump out of the ring. I don't have to use much smartness with him. I'll just corner him and clobber him."

His boldest comment could have come from the mouth of Clay—or from Gorgeous George himself. Addressing Clay directly, Liston said, "If you last three rounds, I'll crawl across the ring and kiss your feet."


During the prelude to the fight, a deeper—and, to many, more troubling—leitmotiv emerged. It was growing more apparent that Clay had become an ex officio, if not an actual member, of the Nation of Islam. His Muslim buddies were coming to the gym, and FBI agents questioned Dundee about Clay's friends.

"I saw Malcolm X in the gym," recalls Dundee. "I was looking to get him out of there, so I went to Rudy"—Clay's brother—"and I said, 'Rudy, tell that guy to leave, will you please, because I don't want no bad write-ups in the paper.'

"He said, 'You go tell him.'

"I said, '*Noooo*.'"

He laughs at the memory today, but at the time the Nation of Islam was seen by white America—and by many blacks—as dangerous and racist, especially at a time of volatile social change. Dr. Martin Luther King, Jr., had delivered his "I have a dream speech"—photographed by Schulke—in August 1963. Vietnam was heating up, and on November 22, just three months before the fight, President Kennedy had been assassinated in Dallas.

Cassius Clay, Sr., had told a *Miami Herald* reporter in early February

1964 that his son had become a Muslim and would declare his faith after the championship fight. With two unsympathetic protagonists—a surly ex-con and a potential social subversive—ticket sales were weak, and the promoters panicked. When Clay said his religion was more important than the championship, the fight was briefly called off.

The official weigh-in was on the morning of the fight, February 25, 1964. Most weigh-ins are pro forma, with the fighters stripping to their underwear, flexing their muscles and stepping on the scales. With Clay, it became a wild scene of manic chaos.

"Strictly bizarre," Dundee says of the weigh-in, thirty-five years later. "It was not planned. It just took hold."

In a word, Clay appeared to go berserk. He was bug-eyed and shouting, jumping up and down, throwing the whole scene into confusion. Wearing a denim jacket with the words BEAR HUNTIN' embroidered on the back, he goaded Liston at every turn, trying to make him believe he—Clay—was truly out of his mind. At one point, Clay lunged at Liston, only to be pulled back by Dundee, Sugar Ray Robinson, and Bundini Brown.

"I'm ready to rumble now!" Clay cried out. "I'm gonna eat you alive!"

"Don't let everyone know what a fool you are," Liston said.

A doctor measured Clay's pulse at 120 beats a minute, when his normal rate was 54, and pronounced him "emotionally unbalanced and in mortal fear."

"He's trying to make jackasses out of us," said a member of the Miami Beach Boxing Commission. He was fined $2,500 on the spot.

Many observers thought Clay was literally scared to death. Nothing so bizarre had ever occurred at a championship fight. It was so shocking, so unexpected, that hardly anyone noticed when, in the midst of the mayhem, Clay turned to his supporters—and winked.

"I'll tell ya," says Dundee, "he should have got the Academy Award for that. You know, the thing was done twice. The first time, we were early, and nobody was there. He did it better the second time."

Amid the turmoil, most people failed to notice that Sonny Liston would step into the ring against a younger man who was as big and powerful as he. Liston, at six-feet-one, weighed 218 pounds. Clay, sculpted in rippling muscle, was actually two inches taller than Liston and entered the fight at 210½ pounds. Liston was a 7-to-1 betting favorite, and many people didn't expect

Clay to last beyond the first round.

"[Cassius] was the calmest cat in the world that night," Dundee recalls. "He was so sure he was going to beat that guy; *I* was so sure he was going to beat that guy. Liston could never lick him."

To everyone's surprise, Clay controlled the pace of the fight, slipping away from Liston's plodding approach. Clay's knifing, twisting punches from odd angles left welts and cuts on the champion's face.

At the end of the fourth round, Clay returned to his corner and complained that he couldn't see.

"I put my pinkie in his eye and put it in my eye," says Dundee. "It burned. Definitely a caustic substance."

"I can't see," Clay said. "There's dirty work afoot!"

To this day, no one is sure what that substance was or how it entered Clay's eyes. Dundee prefers to believe that a liniment applied to Liston's shoulder or face innocently seeped into Clay's eyes during a clinch. It's also possible that someone in Liston's corner illegally "juiced" his gloves to blur Clay's vision and make him vulnerable.

"Cut the gloves off!" Clay demanded. "I can't see!"

"There's no way I'm going to cut them off," Dundee explains today. "How are you going to fight? Then it's an automatic raise-the-other-guy's-hand."

It was the most important moment of the fight, and Dundee seized it. If he hadn't taken charge, the legend of Muhammad Ali might never have been born.

"Get up, get up!" he shouted. He washed Clay's eyes with water, keeping the referee from seeing the danger his fighter was in. When the bell rang for round five, Dundee pushed Clay back into the ring, shouting, "You can't quit now. This is the big one, Daddy! Run!"

Before the fight, Clay had worried that someone might try to drug him or tamper with his water. Some of his Muslim associates had issued warnings about the Mafia and the "white power structure." As the fifth round began, they shouted, "It's a conspiracy," glowering at Dundee, apparently concerned that he—a white Italian-American—had sabotaged his own boxer's chances. With the fight in progress, Dundee reached into the bucket and splashed water into his own eyes to prove it was clean.

During that fifth round, Clay danced around the edge of the ring and along the edge of disaster, holding his left hand out, trying to gauge his distance. Liston attacked but could not put him down. By the end of the round, Clay's vision had cleared. In the next round, the sixth, he took control, hitting Liston at will and opening a deep cut under his left eye.

Students of boxing consider Dundee's performance nearly as remarkable as Clay's. Through his experience and presence of mind, he gave his boxer time to recover and, more important, the will to continue.

"That's what you're there for," says Dundee, "that spur of the moment when you help your fighter. It's that simple, that basic."

After the sixth round, a bleeding, battered Liston trudged back to his corner and said, "That's it." When his trainer tried to put in his mouthpiece for the next round, Liston spat it out. He looked like a man who had aged twenty years in a single night. He sat on his stool and quit the fight, turning over his championship to the young, loud, seemingly demented fighter who had gotten under his skin and inside his head.

When he saw that Liston had given up and that he had won, Clay leaped onto the ropes and mocked the skeptical press seated below. "Eat your words! Eat your words!"

He bounded around the ring, shouting over and over, "I am the king! King of the world! I am the greatest! I shook up the world!"

*When I photographed him the second time, he was a lot bigger, and he didn't look as boyish as he did before. He was real serious about his boxing, but he was always joking and having a lot of fun.*

Drew "Bundini" Brown (wearing cap) was a friend of Clay's who helped keep the laughter going at the Fifth Street Gym. He has been credited with concocting Clay's famous slogan, "Float like a butterfly, sting like a bee."

*When I went to Sonny Liston's camp in Surfside, everything was much*
*more regimented. It was a very serious camp. I didn't have any trouble*
*photographing him, but I never did see him smile. He would always*
*finish his workout jumping rope to his theme song, "Night Train."*
*You could talk to Cassius during his workout,*
*but you couldn't talk to Liston.*

Joe Louis (left), the former heavyweight champion, watches Liston's sparring session.

During a closed-circuit television press conference, Clay brashly predicted that he would defeat the formidable champion, Sonny Liston. As Clay made his comments, Liston can be seen (to the left in the photo above), watching his performance on a different screen.

# CHAPTER FIVE

# Transformation

Two days after the fight, on February 27, 1964, Cassius Clay shook up the world again. In a press conference, a sportswriter directly asked, "Are you a card-carrying member of the Black Muslims?"

" 'Card-carrying,' what does that mean?" Clay answered, before warming to his subject. " 'Black Muslims' is a press word. It's not a legitimate name. The real name is 'Islam.' That means 'peace.'. . .

"You can't condemn a man for wanting peace. If you do, you condemn peace itself."

He concluded with a rustic metaphor: "A rooster crows only when it sees the light. Put him in the dark and he'll never crow. I have seen the light, and I'm crowing."

He was briefly called "Cassius X" until, on March 6, Elijah Muhammad, the spiritual leader of the Nation, bestowed on Clay a new name. From then on, he would be known as Muhammad Ali, meaning "worthy of praise" and "cousin of the prophet."

"Changing my name," Ali said later, "was one of the most important things that happened to me in my life. It freed me from the identity given to my family by slave masters."

---

Having added Sonny Liston to his scrapbook of vanquished opponents (at left), Cassius Clay made an even bolder statement by declaring his faith in the Nation of Islam a couple of days after winning the title.

He was the first prominent African American to become an active member of the Nation of Islam. All these years later, when much of the world has forgotten the name Cassius Clay, it is hard to believe the hatred and outrage that erupted when he changed his name and declared his allegiance to the Nation. For years, sportswriters refused to call him anything but Clay. Politicians denounced Ali—except for a few diehard Southern segregationists who agreed with the Nation's doctrine of racial separation. His own father—Cassius Marcellus Clay, Sr.—was incensed. When boxing opponents such as Ernie Terrell and Floyd Patterson refused to acknowledge Ali's new name, Muhammad beat them cruelly in the ring, shouting between punches, "What's my name?"

For Dundee, who made it a point not to interfere in his fighters' private lives, the name change created a different, if more lighthearted, problem: "What are you going to rhyme with Muhammad?"

A day or two after Ali announced his conversion, Schulke visited him at his house in Overtown. He found a man transformed yet again. Though he still loved to laugh, Ali was more serious, not as loquacious as he had been before. He wore the white shirt and bow tie common to adherents of the Nation of Islam. His new beliefs affected every part of his life. Yet, as he would do throughout his life, he still liked to sit on the front step to chat and joke with the neighborhood kids.

On August 14, 1964, Ali would marry Sonji Roi, the first of his four wives. Less than a year later, he filed for divorce, claiming she did not conform to Muslim teachings.

Among the people hovering around the new champion was Malcolm X, whom Ali had known for two years. Malcolm had helped bring Ali into the Muslim movement, declaring that he would be a greater hero to African Americans than Jackie Robinson. Still in his thirties, Malcolm had spoken of overcoming white oppression "by any means necessary," including violence. Later, he led a dissident Muslim faction that broke away from the authority of the aging Elijah Muhammad.

Malcolm and Ali were close friends for a while, but the rift in the Nation became a rift between them. Elijah Muhammad ordered the young champion

*One thing I regret is that I saw this redheaded black man sitting on the front steps of Cassius's house, talking to him—but I never took a picture. This was during training for the Liston fight. I asked one of the guys, "Who is that? And he said, "Oh, it's some guy from some religion up in Chicago." A few weeks later I realized that it was Malcolm X.*

to return to the orthodox fold, and so he did, breaking off his friendship with Malcolm. Less than a year later, on February 21, 1965, Malcolm was attacked by three gunmen while speaking at a rally in New York and was killed instantly by a blast from a shotgun.

Ali's rematch with Sonny Liston was originally scheduled for November 16, 1964, in Boston. Three days beforehand, Ali had to undergo emergency surgery to ease a serious blockage in his bowel, and the fight was delayed six months. During that time, Malcolm's murder led to rumors that someone might try to assassinate Ali in the ring. The fight was eventually moved to the unlikely town of Lewiston, Maine.

Ali and Liston met for the second, and final, time on May 25, 1965. In the opening round, Ali put Liston on his back and won by a controversial knockout. Many people believed—and some still do—that Liston sold out to gamblers and took a dive. Yet film of the fight clearly shows a short punch from Ali's right hand lifting Liston's feet off the canvas.


As Ali's boxing career advanced, it was becoming ever more clear that his significance would soon reach far beyond the world of sports. In 1960, while still in high school in Louisville, the young Cassius Clay had registered for the military draft. On January 24, 1964, just a month before his first fight with Liston, he was ordered to report to a recruiting station in the Miami suburb of Coral Gables to take the armed forces' standardized tests. He did poorly in the mathematics and language sections and was classified 1-Y—"not qualified" for military service.

"I said I was the greatest, not the smartest," he sheepishly explained.

Within two years, the Vietnam War had turned hot, and the U.S. government stepped up the military draft. On Valentine's Day, 1966, Ali's attorney formally requested that he be exempt from military service because of his Muslim belief in nonviolence. Within three days, his request was turned down, and he was reclassified 1-A. Reporters camped on his lawn in Miami, begging for a comment. The phone rang again and again. Peeved by the entire scene, Ali blurted out, "Man, I ain't got no quarrel with them Vietcong."

Three decades later, the unguarded statement of a twenty-four-year-old sums up much of the nation's view of the war in Vietnam. But in 1966, Ali's comment made the front pages throughout the country. He was denounced by columnists and congressmen, and the FBI began an investigation. Ali appealed the draft board's decision, but by April 28, 1967, his options had come to an end. On that day, citing his religious beliefs, he refused to be inducted into the army. Within an hour, his heavyweight title was withdrawn.

In short order, he was convicted of draft evasion and sentenced to five years in prison. His passport was confiscated, preventing him from fighting anywhere in the world.

With the antiwar movement gaining momentum, Ali was propelled onto a larger, more controversial public stage. Supporters of the nation's war effort accused him of being a coward, but bravery was not the real issue. As a celebrity, he would probably not have seen the front lines in Vietnam—and, in any case, he had already shown plenty of courage in the ring. Ali's refusal to serve was a matter of religious belief and private principle from which he never backed down, not even in the face of retribution and scorn.

Through it all, Ali remained serene, even when the championship that he had strived to achieve since he was a boy had been taken away. He was twenty-five years old at the time and would not fight again until he was almost twenty-nine. During those years of forced exile, the peak of Ali's ability and earning power came and went.

"They robbed him," says Angelo Dundee, still upset three decades after the fact. "The idiots that robbed him ought to be ashamed of themselves. They took a man's living away from him. That was the most terrible thing they could do."

Ali appealed his conviction, and for four years his case wound its way through the courts. Through this long ordeal, something unexpected came to pass: The world around Ali began to change—or perhaps he changed the world—and people came to recognize him as a man of dignity and integrity. Nothing—not even the force of the U.S. government or the loss of his livelihood—could make him waver in his beliefs. America and the world grew to respect Muhammad Ali as a man who would not betray his own ideals. With understanding came public honor and, eventually, love.

He never did serve his prison sentence, yet Ali remained under constant surveillance by various intelligence agencies for years. The only time he was actually behind bars came in December 1968, when he spent a week in jail in Miami for driving without a license. Even during those volatile times, the sentence seemed unduly harsh for such a petty offense. In 1971, his draft-evasion case finally reached the Supreme Court, which unanimously overturned his conviction.

The year before, in 1970, a court in New York allowed him to return to boxing, ruling that men convicted of far more serious crimes were allowed to box. When he began his training, he came back to the place where his long journey had begun. Muhammad Ali climbed the stairs and stepped back into the timeless rhythms of the Fifth Street Gym, where his sweat would drip again upon the floor, and where a true champion would rise once more.

---

A few days after the Liston fight, Schulke encountered a more serious Clay (at right), lunching at his modest home in Miami.

Reciting a comical poem praising his performance as boxing's newest king, Clay hadn't entirely given up his old, jovial manner.

*When I saw him again a few days after the Liston fight, he was very different—and very serious. He was on his way to a Muslim rally; that's why he was wearing the bow tie. He wasn't joking and kidding around the way he used to.*

*I got lots of pictures of Cassius talking to children. The only time*
*he lightened up was when he went out to see the neighborhood kids—he*
*loved them. He would sit on the front steps and talk to*
*all of the children who came up to him.*

## ABOUT THE PHOTOGRAPHER

FLIP SCHULKE has been one of America's premier photojournalists for more than forty-five years. A native of New Ulm, Minnesota, and a graduate of Macalester College in St. Paul, Schulke moved to Miami in the 1950s, where he developed specialties in underwater photography, auto racing, the space program, and the history of the Berlin Wall. Through his close friendship with Dr. Martin Luther King, Jr., he became best known as one of the leading chroniclers of the Southern civil-rights movement. He covered nearly every major civil-rights story in the South from the 1950s until Dr. King's assassination in 1968.

For many years, Schulke was a contract photographer for *Life* magazine. His work has also appeared in *National Geographic* magazine, *Sports Illustrated*, *Time*, *Newsweek*, *The Saturday Evening Post*, *Der Stern*, and numerous other publications. Schulke has won dozens of national photojournalism awards, including first-prize honors for Picture of the Year. In 1986, he was presented with the first annual New York State Martin Luther King, Jr., Medal by Governor Mario Cuomo. In 1995, he received the Crystal Eagle Award from the National Press Photographers Association for his lifelong documentation of the civil-rights movement.

Schulke lectures frequently throughout the country on photojournalism, the civil-rights struggle of the 1960s, and his friendship with Dr. King. He is the author of five previous books. During his career, Schulke has taken more than 500,000 photographs, all of which are in his personal archives. He has the largest independent collection of civil-rights photographs in the world, containing more than 11,000 images. His archives will eventually be housed in the Center for American History at the University of Texas at Austin. A duplicate set, on disk, will reside at Macalester College in St. Paul. He and his wife, Donna, live in West Palm Beach, Florida.

ABOUT THE AUTHOR

MATT SCHUDEL is a native of North Loup, Nebraska, and a graduate of the University of Nebraska and the University of Virginia. He has been a staff member of *U.S. News & World Report* and *The Washington Post* and is currently a senior writer for the Sunday magazine of the *Sun-Sentinel* in Fort Lauderdale, Florida.

*I saw Muhammad again a few years ago in Miami. I had the pictures*
*with me, and I showed them to him. He remembered everything.*
*The guy's mind is as sharp as a tack. When I showed him a print of*
*the two of us in boxing trunks at the pool, he signed it,*
**To Flip, from Muhammad Ali, aka Cassius Clay.**